YOUR KNOWLEDGE HAS VALUE

AF130473

- We will publish your bachelor's and master's thesis, essays and papers

- Your own eBook and book - sold worldwide in all relevant shops

- Earn money with each sale

Upload your text at www.GRIN.com and publish for free

Performance effects of application programming interfaces (API). What is the impact of distinct design choices and value creation strategies?

Jun-Ying Poon

Bibliographic information published by the German National Library:

The German National Library lists this publication in the National Bibliography; detailed bibliographic data are available on the Internet at http://dnb.dnb.de.

ISBN: 9783346427762
This book is also available as an ebook.

© GRIN Publishing GmbH
Nymphenburger Straße 86
80636 München

All rights reserved

Print and binding: Books on Demand GmbH, Norderstedt, Germany
Printed on acid-free paper from responsible sources.

The present work has been carefully prepared. Nevertheless, authors and publishers do not incur liability for the correctness of information, notes, links and advice as well as any printing errors.

GRIN web shop: https://www.grin.com/document/1015092

Performance Effects of Application Programming Interfaces based on Design and Strategy Choices

SELECTED ISSUES IN DIGITALIZATION
SEMINAR PAPER

Submitted to

Chair of Interorganizational Information Systems

University of Göttingen

In
01/2021
(WS 20/21)

Academic Program:
B.Sc. Business Information Systems

Abstract

The rise of digital platforms in recent years induced a substantial emergence of Application Programming Interfaces (APIs) at business organizations. By connecting two parties with mutual interests, APIs facilitate digital collaboration and generate network effects beneficial to both. This literature review examines a research conducted on the performance effects of APIs. It measures the potential impact of distinct design choices and value creation strategies on the commercial outcome and pervasion of an API. The results suggest that API design must be deliberately coordinated with the strategy of value creation in order to achieve desirable business objectives. The findings are demonstrated with a case study on open banking as a practical example. Moreover, the paper is contextualized with two related journal articles, validating and extending the insights found.

Table of Content

List of Figures

List of Tables

1 Introduction

Over the last decade, an increasing number of organizations have established Application Programming Interfaces (APIs) to complement their business. While the website ProgrammableWeb listed
361 public web APIs in their directory in 2007, this number increased to over 22,000 as of 2020 (ProgrammableWeb Research Center). A public API facilitates the digital communication between two
applications over a network and enables a firm to connect their system to the infrastructure of another organization. By providing data or functionality using a public interface, a firm establishes an
alternative channel to distribute his services. Developers at third-party vendors can then access the
digital data under the guidance of the API documentary without the necessity to comprehend the
internal workings and algorithms (Ghazawneh and Henfridsson 2013).

Despite the increasing significance of APIs, the academic literature to date provides sparse insights
about the potential impact of API design on the performance outcomes thereof. In their paper "Fostering Value Creation with Digital Platforms: A Unified Theory of the Application Programming Interface Design" (Wulf and Blohm 2020), the authors close this gap in knowledge by investigating the
interaction effects of API design and means of value creation on the *return on investment* (*ROI*) and
the *diffusion* of the API. They construct a theoretical framework on which they conduct a survey with
API providers and several qualitative analyses to reach regression analyses. They also contribute to
current scientific knowledge by conceptualizing the characteristics of three distinct API types and two
value creation mechanisms. To support the findings of the paper, an example from the field of open
banking is illustrated (Kyprianides 2018) and put into the framework introduced by Wulf and Blohm.
The research is further extended by two closely related journal articles (Aitamurto and Lewis 2013;
Tan et al. 2020), adding both concurrent and novel perspectives to the research question.

This literature review proceeds with an explanation of the practical and theoretical motivation as
well as the leading question behind the research. It then elaborates on the fundamental concepts
required for the analyses, followed by the hypotheses, methodologies and results of the study. Upon
a review of the theoretical contributions and practical implications of the findings, the paper is further discussed on the basis of the exemplary case study and two related researches. The paper con-
cludes by commenting on prospective fields of future research.

2 Motivation

The research of Wulf and Blohm (2020) was driven by both practical and theoretical underlying rationales, which are laid out in the following two subsections.

2.1 Practical motivation

A provider introducing an API strives to attract and integrate third-party developers by enabling access to company-internal information technology (IT) resources or functionality. For this endeavor to succeed, the authors suggest that the API must be deliberately designed to match the general business objectives intended by the provider. It must also align with the demands of not only the third-party vendors, but also the end consumers of the API provider. While the significance of API design for the competitiveness on the market is often undervalued (Iyer and Subramaniam 2015), the research will show that the extent to which an API performs on the market is largely dependent on the chosen design and overall strategy.

Furthermore, incentives are to be provided for the external developers to initiate and maintain a relationship with the API provider. If a provider fails to factor in the business objectives of the developers, the resulting API is potentially rendered unattractive for the third parties. Wulf and Blohm deem this a necessary aspect to consider when establishing a public API.

2.2 Theoretical motivation

The authors also address theoretical issues in academic literature to date as another basis for their research. Papers on APIs have so far chosen to holistically analyze sets of multiple APIs in organizations or platforms (such as Benlian et al. 2015) but has not observed APIs as individual units. While there are viable results related to API design and associated performance effects, the applicability of any research finding on an API level is largely restricted. By focusing their study on individual APIs, Wulf and Blohm resolve this issue and make a novel contribution to API literature.

Also, the design and architecture of APIs was researched in a detached context until now. The paper identifies three clusters of APIs employed by platform providers and maps those to three API *archetypes*: *professional services*, *mediation services* and *open asset services*. Existing literature has studied each of these types extensively, but only in an isolated environment and not in a uniform manner. By applying an integrative approach to all three API *archetypes*, the authors respond to a call for a combined theory on different API choices and respective outcomes (Yoo et al. 2010).

Furthermore, two distinct mechanisms of value creation are conceptualized, *economies of scope in production* (Krishnan and Gupta 2001) on the one hand and *economies of scope in innovation* (Adner and Kapoor 2010) on the other hand. The authors could not identify any prior research on both mechanisms, prompting them to fill that gap in literature themselves.

2.3 Research question

The paper of Wulf and Blohm aims to advance API research on multiple open topics. It will define and characterize three distinct types of API design (namely *professional services, mediation services* and *open asset services*) and two value creation mechanisms (*economies of scope in production* and *in innovation*). Taking into consideration those two concepts, the interaction effects of both variables on either *return on investment (ROI)* or *diffusion* is computed, with *diffusion* comprising adaption and awareness of the API within the external developer community. Simply put, the *ROI* and the level of *diffusion* are investigated dependent on a given combination of API *archetype* and *value creation mechanism*. These correlations are estimated with ordinal logistic and negative binomial regression analyses. Using the results of the analysis, the authors approach their research question whether APIs of differing *archetypes* should be deployed in conjunction with an appropriate *value creation mechanism* in order to reach the organizational objective of either *ROI* or *diffusion*.

The research is restricted in that only public, openly specified APIs accessible over the internet are considered. Private APIs used internally within an enterprise are not investigated, as those do not provide the capability of creating external revenue or adoption (Curbera et al. 2003). Also, only for-profit organizations are included in the analyses to ensure a general pursuit of profit maximization.

3 Fundamental concepts

To establish a common conception of the terminology and theories used in the paper, this chapter will explain core concepts and terms that are essential to the understanding of the main model.

3.1 Application Programming Interface (API), platform and design characteristics

An API is defined as an interface that external applications can connect to without knowing the interior mechanics. APIs "enable interfaces, services, and applications to connect seamlessly with one another, making digital content accessible between a wide range of independent applications" (Bodle 2011, p. 325). They grant design capabilities to developers and act as platform boundary resources. Boundary resources are regulations of the interaction between the owner and the developers, allowing owners to maintain control over the ecosystem (Ghazawneh and Henfridsson 2013).

A digital platform provides a main functionality that can be expanded with third party modules, subsystems adding functionality to the software (Tiwana et al. 2010). The distinct choices regarding the design of a platform can be attributed to either one of two categories: platform architecture and platform governance. A graphical representation of the following structure is shown in Figure 3 in the appendix.

3.1.1 Platform architecture

Wulf and Blohm define architecture as the *partitioning* and *systems integration* of a platform. *Partitioning* describes whether the platform is merely supplying access to data or infrastructure (Demirkan and Delen 2013) or if it also provides more complex functionality, like handling information for business processes, referred to as *function* hereafter (Xue et al. 2017). It moreover describes whether the API acts as a distribution channel for customer-directed services by providing *end customer access* and marketing capabilities to third party developers, the alternative being that the vendors do not encounter the customer base at all (Smedlund 2012).

Systems integration addresses whether the provider interconnects with the developers via a *multi-channel access* and to what extent *security* safeguarding the platform and infrastructure is in place. The API-based access to a service is considered multi-channel if the functionality is originally offered in a software-based or web-based environment, making the access via the API a supplemental mode of consumption (Nuettgens and Iskender 2008). The *security* characteristic indicates the presence of data encryption methods to minimize the threat of platform breaches, as security concerns may hinder prospective developers from participating (Lin and Chen 2012).

3.1.2 Platform governance

Three characteristics compose the governance of a platform according to the authors: *decision rights, control* and *pricing*. The *decision rights* of a platform owner are upheld if the *end customer relationship* is maintained (Smedlund 2012) – else, the owner relinquishes that right to the vendors. *Platform control* is exercised when the provider installs *user authorization* to individually allow or restrict access to certain parts of the platform (Benzell et al. 2019). In contrast, minimizing authorization facilitates ease of use and potentially attracts more developers. The *pricing* of a platform can take three distinct forms: *subscription-based charging*, where developers are billed on a periodic basis for continuing usage (Zimmermann et al. 2016), *transaction-based charging*, where costs are incurred for each API consumption (Nuettgens and Iskender 2008), and *revenue sharing*, where third party vendors are paid a proportion of the earnings generated by their developed service (Parker and Van Alstyne 2005). A provider can also aim to assemble a large developer community by offering the consumption for free.

3.2 API archetypes

The illustrated characteristics of architecture and governance will now be used to differentiate between three API *archetypes*, as defined by Wulf and Blohm: *professional services, mediation services* and *open asset services*. Providing access to own IT resources while charging a fee for the consumption is defined as *professional services* (Xin and Levina 2008). These service modules are usually also accessible using a proprietary software or a browser, whereas the API access facilitates easy integration into the vendors' IT infrastructure. The Google Maps API is an example of a *professional service*. Platforms connecting two sides of a market are called *mediation services*, enabling external vendors to develop additional services for the end consumers of the platform (Niculescu et al. 2018). By providing platform resources like business development and marketing, the vendors are incited to innovate. One example is Facebook Graph which enables developers to read and write data on the Facebook platform (Facebook for Developers). *Open asset services* give access to IT resources at no charge, while interface and governance standards minimize the effort of integration (Rudmark 2013). These are usually data services without a need for user authorization. The New York Times for example facilitates free article search with their API (NYT Developer Network).

3.3 Mechanisms of value creation

The authors define two means of creating values with APIs, both grounded on costs reduction: *economies of scope in production* and *in innovation*. When two market players create an intermediate and the subsequent end product in separation, it is potentially cheaper to produce those in mutual collaboration. This is what the paper calls *economies of scope in production*, the optimization of a production process by vertically integrating the stages of value creation (Panzar and Willig 1981). The *economies of scope in innovation* on the other hand describes the cost-reduced innovation process of two products when joint innovation is less costly than separate innovation (Gawer 2014).

3.4 Measurements of API performance

To assess how well an API performs, two figures are introduced that will ultimately serve as the two dependent variables of the study: the *return on investment (ROI)* and the *diffusion* of the API. The *ROI* measures the net profit (i.e. revenue) rendered by the API relative to the total costs incurred during its development and operation (Im and Workman 2004). The generation of revenue is also referred to as *value appropriation* and is feasible either directly by charging consumption fees or indirectly by increasing the attractiveness of the main product (Henfridsson and Bygstad 2013). *Diffusion* is a composite measurement of *awareness* and *adoption* and indicates how well-known an API is among developers (Setia et al. 2012). A greater *diffusion* tends to bolster the innovational strength of the provider (Chesbrough and Appleyard 2007).

4 Research Approach

To investigate the effects of API *archetype* and *value creation mechanism* on *ROI* and *diffusion* of APIs, Wulf and Blohm construct four hypotheses and test these with a variety of methods.

4.1 Hypotheses

In essence, the hypotheses claim that the design of an API must align with the intended *value crea-tion mechanism* (*economies of scope*) of the provider in order to achieve the business objective of either *return on investment* or *diffusion*. The hypothesized correlations are modeled in Figure 1.

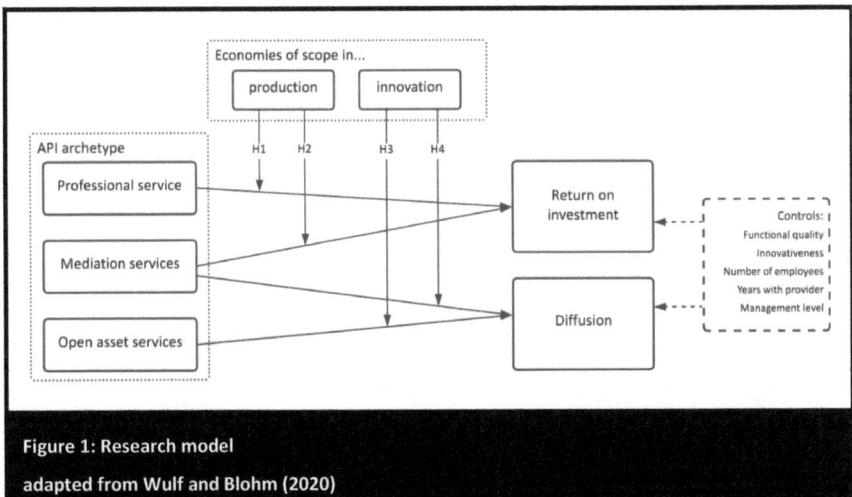

Figure 1: Research model

adapted from Wulf and Blohm (2020)

Hypothesis 1 (H1) states that the *ROI* of an API is positively affected when the design shows charac-teristics of a *professional service* while the provider targets *economies of scope in production*. Such APIs intend to generate revenue by charging developers for the provision of services integrable in their own applications (Benlian et al. 2011). By modularizing the offered IT resources, these assets can be implemented even in complex and customized application landscapes of third parties (Xin and Levina 2008). Wulf and Blohm argue that *professional services* directly foster *ROI* as they establish a novel revenue channel with relatively low investments. However, they are not designed to increase *diffusion* as they do not strive to maximize reach among developers.

Hypothesis 2 (H2) also relates the provision of *mediation services* in conjunction with *economies of scope in production* to an increased *ROI*. Providers can attract third-party developers by facilitating easy integration into their apps, prompting them to enrich the platform with complementary ser-vices. This pulls in end customer revenue (e.g. by charging higher fees), which in turn raises the *ROI* (Song et al. 2018).

Hypothesis 3 (H3) postulates a higher *diffusion* of *open asset services* APIs when *economies of scope in innovation* are in place. The provider grants free access to internal resources in easily integrable modules, stimulating externals to forge innovations (Ghazawneh and Henfridsson 2013). This is further incited as the maintenance effort and operational costs are very low for the developers (Kuk and Davies 2011). Trying to reach a developer base as large as possible, the goal of an open asset API is the *diffusion* thereof. As it comes with no pricing model, the platform does not target monetary benefits, but rather value generation in the innovational sense (Chesbrough and Appleyard 2007).

Hypothesis 4 (H4) associates *mediation services* in *economies of scope in innovation* with *diffusion* as well. As third-party innovations leverage the value of the platform, there is a significant motivation to attract more developers. In order to do so, the owner may consider sharing parts of the generated revenue with the vendors (Parker and Van Alstyne 2005). Thus, the authors expect a greater *diffusion* for *mediation services* in *economies of scope in innovation*.

4.2 Methodology and results

To test the validity of the constructed hypotheses, the objective of Wulf and Blohm's research is to reach regression analyses with API *ROI* and *diffusion* respectively as dependent variable. In order to set up these analyses, the authors must define each required variable and gather the associated data. For a full graphical breakdown of the research process, please find Figure 4 in the appendix.

4.2.1 Data acquisition

To obtain data of active APIs, product managers of 2950 for-profit API providers were invited to a survey, to which 152 responded. The survey was conducted to assess *ROI*, the *value creation mechanism* intended by the provider and *controlling variables (functional quality, service innovativeness, number of employees, affiliation with provider, job tenure)*. These variables are potentially significant regressors and are necessarily included – else, their correlation with *ROI* or *diffusion* may be falsely attributed to other regressors, causing an omitting variable bias (Podsakoff et al. 2003).

For *ROI*, the product managers were prompted to rate on a scale from 1 to 5 how well the *ROI* performed relative to the original objectives set by the organization. Regarding the *value creation mechanisms*, the authors developed three questions each with guidance from prior literature. A provider was deemed to act within *economies of scope in production* when the API was highly rated (again from 1 to 5) for the capability of flexible integration, of adaption and of deep integration into third party infrastructure. On the other hand, *economies of scope in innovation* was assumed if the findings indicated that the API "allows to tap the inventive capacities [...], to exploit the creative potential of [third parties] and to enhance an API provider's innovation capabilities" (Wulf and Blohm 2020, pp. 262-263). To merge both sets of questions into single factors ranging from 1 to 5, they applied exploratory and confirmatory factor analysis which are methods to deduce one underlying factor from multiple related variables. The results of the analysis are significant and thus legitimate the use of single variables to represent either mechanism.

After capturing *ROI* and *value creation mechanisms* for 152 providers, qualitative analysis was conducted on prior API literature to define the various characteristics and types of API design. By aggregating concepts found in other papers, the authors theorized nine traits (as for instance *user authorization* and *revenue sharing*) and three *archetypes* (*professional services, mediation services* and *open asset services*) of API design. With the characteristics defined in a coding scheme, the documentations and websites of all 152 surveyed APIs were qualitatively analyzed and coded accordingly (an API without encryption for instance would be coded *0* in *security*). To ascertain the *archetype* of the characterized APIs, cluster analyses verified the theoretically devised typologies and classified each API to their respective group. Simply put, cluster analyses find distinct groups of entities with similar attributes and assign any entity to the closest resembling group (Leisch 2006). For every characteristic, the percentage of APIs with that trait within each cluster was calculated. A percentage above 50% determines it as a common characteristic for that cluster. The results are as follows in **Table 1**.

Table 1. Implementation of API design characteristics by cluster based on Wulf and Blohm (2020)					
API Design Characteristic	**Professional Services**		**Mediation Services**		**Open Asset Services**	
	Percentage (in %)	Archetype (0 or 1)	Percentage (in %)	Archetype (0 or 1)	Percentage (in %)	Archetype (0 or 1)
End Customer Access	0	0	66.67	1	4.35	0
Multi-Channel Access	72.55	1	59.26	1	100	1
End Customer Relationship	0.98	0	66.67	1	0	0
Function	92.16	1	88.89	1	0	0
Subscription-based Charge	97.06	1	11.11	0	0	0
Transaction-based Charge	96.08	1	7.41	0	4.35	0
User Authorization	98.04	1	100	1	65.22	1
Security	68.63	1	74.07	1	21.74	0
Revenue sharing	0	0	18.52	0	0	0
N (in %)	**67.10**		**17.76**		**15.13**	

Professional services generate revenue by granting *user authorization* to third party vendors only against a *subscription-based* or *transaction-based charge*. While the business process *functionality* is also accessible with a proprietary software or a browser, the API facilitates direct and encrypted (*security*) integration into the external system. *Mediation services* maintain the *end customer relationship* but also provide *end customer access* to third parties, establishing a two-sided platform. This is the only archetype that potentially involves *revenue sharing*, while direct fees are scarcely charged. *Open asset services* are usually limited to infrastructure or data access and do not include any *function*. It is free of charge and spurs open innovation by third parties. The API is always an alternative way of consumption (*multi-channel access*).

For every API, the difference in each characteristic is aggregated and calculated as the distance to the archetype, scaled from 0 to 1. Subtracting that distance from 1 yields a similarity measure. A *professional services* value of 0.9 for example indicates an API very similar to that archetype.

The *diffusion* of an API is compound of *adoption* and *awareness*. To measure *adoption,* the authors gathered the number of repositories using that API on Github. For *awareness*, they counted comments on Stack Overflow related to the API and the number of followers on ProgrammableWeb. These measures were combined to the single variable *diffusion* using non-negative matrix factorization, a technique similar to factor analysis (Lee and Seung 2001).

4.2.2 Regression analyses

To investigate the interaction effects of the API *archetype* and the *value creation mechanism,* Wulf and Blohm set up an ordinal logistic regression for *ROI* and a negative binomial regression for *diffusion*. The ordinal logistic regression accounts for the discrete nature of *ROI* which is a whole number from 1 to 5. It predicts the probability to attain a given *ROI* level or higher depending on the independent variables. Two models were computed (for full results see Table 2 in the appendix): Model 1a without and Model 1b including the interaction terms *economies of scope in production * professional services* and *economies of scope in production * mediation services*. The interaction terms are the multiplication of both variables. If, for instance, an API is 0.8 in *mediation services* (high similarity to the archetype) and 4 in *economies of scope in production,* the term Is 3.2 for that API. While the first model did not yield any significant findings, the second model deems both interaction terms to be significant at the 5% level. The coefficients are positive (0.45 and 0.37), indicating that with any increase in either interaction term, the *ROI* is more likely to attain a high level ceteris paribus. As the analysis could prove that the *ROI* of an API is in fact positively related to the interaction of *economies of scope in production* with the *professional services* and *mediation services* archetypes respectively, the authors accept Hypothesis 1 and 2 at a 95% confidence level.

The variable *diffusion* is derived from count data which are prone to overdispersion, a phenomenon where the variance of the sample is greater than theoretically expected (Harrell 2015). To account for this, the authors deployed a negative binomial regression model. Another two models were computed (see Table 3): Model 2a without and Model 2b including the interaction terms *economies of scope in innovation * open asset services* and *economies of scope In innovation * mediation services*. The first model again does not yield any significant finding, while the second model computed a positive, statistically significant coefficient (0.45) of the interaction term *economies of scope in innovation * open asset services*. This implies that an API with high similarity to *open asset services* and a high level of *economies of scope in innovation* is expected to increase the *diffusion* ceteris paribus, confirming Hypothesis 3. The coefficient of *economies of scope in innovation * mediation services* was not found to be significant, prompting the authors to reject Hypothesis 4.

5   Contribution and implications

The paper of Wulf and Blohm fill research gaps in both practical and theoretical regards, as already laid out in Chapter 2.

5.1   Theoretical contribution

Prior literature is scattered in that only APIs of a specific design are studied without considering the entire range of distinct API types. The authors condense that literature into one common theory and establish three API design archetypes: *professional services, mediation services* and *open asset services*. By providing a unified design theory based on existing papers, they answer the call for additional research (Yoo et al. 2010). Also, prior research only examines the performance of the whole organization or platform associated with an API (Benzell et al. 2019; Song et al. 2017), impeding the attribution of performance effects to individual APIs. The authors break with that pattern by conducting the study on a single API level and thus expand the research on API performance effects. They also extend the literature by concurrently studying two *value creation mechanisms*, namely *economies of scope in production* and *economies of scope in innovation*.

The main contribution of the paper is the formulation of consequences of the choice of API design on performance outcomes. The paper demonstrates the combination of API-specific design *archetype* and intended *value creation mechanism* exerts a significant impact on the *ROI* and *diffusion* thereof.

5.2   Practical contribution

The study bears implications regarding API design in practice. When establishing an API, a provider should coordinate the design choices with the targeted *value creation mechanism* and the overall objective set by the organization. For *professional services,* the solution can potentially raise the *ROI* by ensuring that the solution is easily integrated and adaptable to third-party systems. In like manner, facilitating the platform integration may generate higher direct or indirect revenue for *mediation services*. In the case of *open asset services*, a high level of *diffusion* can be reached when the API succeeds in attracting developers for joint innovation and exploits the external innovational strength.

Furthermore, the authors suggest that providers reassess their business objectives in accordance with their value creation approach. If the platform targets *economies of scope in production*, transaction-based or subscription-based fees may be advisable to generate revenue. In case of *economies of scope in innovation*, the provider should focus on attracting external developers to spur innovation.

6 Further research

This chapter involves additional papers of contemporary API literature and contextually relates them to the main article by Wulf and Blohm. On the basis of these papers, an actual productive example will be examined, and academic advances linked to the research conducted by the authors.

6.1 Practical example

For the productive example, the concept of open banking will be investigated jointly with a case study of the introduction of APIs at the Hellenic Bank, a bank based in Cyprus with a strong digital focus. Having operated their banking services via web and mobile interfaces for a number of years, they adopted an "API-first approach" (Kyprianides 2018, p. 57) in April 2017.

This extension in strategy was spurred by the introduction of the PSD2 directive in 2016 by the European Commission, which paved the way to an API economy in the banking industry (Farrow 2020a). PSD2 is a set of regulations with the goal to form a marketplace with newly founded competitors. In short, it decrees banks to grant *third-party providers* (*TPP*) access to payment and bank information. This enables *account information service providers* (*AISP*) to read data like transaction history or account information of end customers. They also enable *payment initiation service providers* (*PISP*) to read and write data in order to handle payments (Farrow 2020a). The interactions are shown in Figure 2.

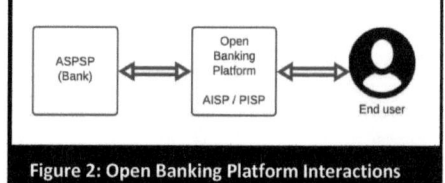

Figure 2: Open Banking Platform Interactions (adapted from Farrow, 2020a)

The PSD2 directive allows third party developers to build applications and services using open APIs, facilitating significant potential for innovation growth in the market (Constantinides et al. 2018). *AISP*s and *PISP*s are given the opportunity to create revenue by innovating on novel products based on improved insights. *Account servicing payments service providers* (*ASPSP*), which are conventional banks in the broad sense, increase customer interaction as well as account and transaction volumes channeled by the value-added services from *TPP*s. Furthermore, they can drive in direct revenue by monetizing the consumption of the API (Farrow 2020b).

Hellenic Bank offers APIs for a number of functionalities: authentication, single payments, mass payments, products list, account details and account reporting. As laid out in the following, all three archetypes (Wulf and Blohm 2020) are represented in their API landscape. The bank established a platform allowing developers to submit new products and developments. Once approved, these applications are available in a proprietary app store where customers can explore these offerings. As of 2018, a total of 395 developers have created 155 applications, with a transaction volume of 78 million euro handled by 153 thousand API calls (Kyprianides 2018). The bank also cross-sells the prod-ucts in the marketplace and thus provides *end customer access* to the vendors while maintaining the *end customer relationship*. This is a direct representation of the *mediation services* archetype as ven-dors and end users are connected on a two-sided digital platform.

Using an open banking API, business partners such as insurance firms are able to create and manage complementary products. This omits the need to individually implement a solution for every business partner, reducing infrastructure and transaction costs for both parties by operating on one single digital platform (Farrow 2020b). This synergy is a distinct example for *economies of scope in produc-tion*, as the vertical integration of two value creation stages cuts the collective production costs com-pared to separate production. Another paper on open banking APIs (Zachariadis and Ozcan 2016) claims that by increasing the integration of a banking platform, a provider leverages the user interac-tion and thereby profitability in the mid term. This verifies the second hypothesis of Wulf and Blohm that a *mediation services* API in *economies of scope in production* is more likely to attain a higher *ROI*. Zachariadis and Ozcan also claims that by establishing an innovative banking platform early on, it is possible to trigger a reciprocal cycle of attracting a large customer base owing to an increasing num-ber of third-party services, who in turn attract more developers. A cycle of that kind would conform with the fourth hypothesis (*mediation services* in *economies of scope in innovation* also leverage the API *diffusion*) which Wulf and Blohm were, in fact, unable to validate.

In addition to the two-sided platform, the bank also enables corporate customers to connect their Enterprise-Resource-Planning (ERP) system with the API, facilitating payment orders from within the system. The API also provides the status of the account and transactions and overrides the necessity for manual bank statement exports. While the access was offered for free as of 2018, it was in con-sideration to introduce consumption fees (Kyprianides 2018). In that case, the API would be arche-typal of *professional services*, as the provider will increase *ROI* by directly generating income.

Lastly, Hellenic Bank operates an API for free product information accessible without a formal rela-tionship with the bank. This encourages third parties to come up with innovative service offerings, making that API an *open asset service*. Another example of this archetype is the Open Bank Project started in Germany, an open source banking API that allows any third party to contribute and inno-vate on the platform (Zachariadis and Ozcan 2016).

6.2 Role in discourse

This subchapter extends the findings derived by Wulf and Blohm by drawing upon further research related to the introduced concepts. This includes papers on pricing decisions on two-sided platforms (Tan et al. 2020) and the effect of open APIs in digital journalism (Aitamurto and Lewis 2013).

6.2.1   Pricing decisions on two-sided platforms

The article "Platform Pricing and Investment to Drive Third-Party Value Creation in Two-Sided Networks" (Tan et al. 2020) discusses revenue mechanisms for owners of two-sided platforms and directly relates to the implications made concerning *mediation services*. The purpose of the paper is to give guidance on the coordination of pricing decisions and investments in platform integration and to emphasize the importance thereof for the success of the platform. Tan et al. advocate the significance of well-designed APIs and associate the usefulness of a two-sided platform with the number of integrated third-party services and customers.

To build a theoretical model of the strategic interdependency between integration investment and pricing policies on a two-sided platform, the authors conducted a mathematical analysis. Upon modeling all relevant variables in formal equations, they derived lemmas for the optimal integration investment, the optimal consumer price and the optimal participation fee for third-party providers. A substantial finding claims that by investing in integration, the conventional pricing theory that the price for one side of the market should decrease when the utility for the other side increases is no longer valid. Instead, if utility for either side increases through improved integration, it might be optimal for the platform owner to increase both consumer prices and third-party participation fees. This appropriates some of the increase in value for consumers, but also counterbalances the reduction in integration costs for third parties. The concept of raising revenue by charging the vendors is an extension of Hypothesis 2, which postulates a higher *ROI* for *mediation services* in *economies of scope in production*. Wulf and Blohm ground the higher *ROI* in an increase of end customer fees, as their utility is improved in the presence of third-party offerings. Tan et al. on the other hand theorize an increased revenue drawn from both sides of the platform.

The models also impose various conditions regarding pricing. If the content price charged by the content provider from the end consumer is low while consumer utility is high, a larger increase in consumer price is optimal. With a high content price and lower consumer utility, it is advisable to increase the participation fee to a larger extent. The models also compare a platform with high integration capabilities but low standalone value against a platform with low integration capabilities but high standalone value. When the consumer utility from the provided content is high, the platform with high integration investments captures a larger market share despite the lower standalone value. This in turn addresses Hypothesis 4, stating that a platform with the characteristics of *mediation services* is also capable of increasing *diffusion*. The difference is that the original hypothesis assumed the platform to target *economies of scope in innovation*, while this paper examines the effect of reinforced integration which Wulf and Blohm define as *economies of scope in production*.

6.2.2   Open APIs in digital journalism

The paper "Open innovation in digital journalism: Examining the impact of Open APIs at four news organizations" (Aitamurto and Lewis 2013) discusses APIs as innovation drivers and relates to the main paper by elaborating on the concept of *open asset services*. It examines the potential value of open innovation in the journalism industry and focuses on APIs providing information content. The authors undertook a multiple-case study on the news organizations The New York Times, The Guardian, USA Today and NPR by conducting interviews with at least one API developer at each firm. They subsequently performed qualitative analyses to code the discussions and used a theoretical framework to determine which aspects of open innovation were implemented in each organization. The main finding of the research comprises two substantial effects of open APIs: improvements in research and development and a potential for new revenue streams.

Releasing access to news articles and other journalistic data entices external developers to experiment with innovations incorporating that data. Internal developers at the newspaper can build on those experiments and exploit good ideas to develop proprietary products, a behavior exemplary of *economies of scope in innovation* as defined by Wulf and Blohm. In addition to saving resources for prototyping, they can also use the third parties to find previously undiscovered markets. Niche products such as reader applications for sparsely distributed operating systems target potential user bases the organization would have otherwise overlooked. The authors show that the innovative potential of the interfaces attracts many developers – the open API of The Guardian, for instance, counts 4000 registered developers and 2000 connected applications. This phenomenon reflects *Hypothesis 3* of the main paper that an *open asset service* in *economies of scope in innovation* increases *diffusion*.

The expansion of the product portfolio of a newspaper also creates potential for commercialization. The Guardian offers three levels of API consumption, with the third level entailing full access to more than a million articles for an appropriate fee. This type of commercial license is also available at USA Today, as they charge developers for expanded access to their content. That implies a potential raise in *ROI* for *open asset services* in *economies of scope in innovation*, a relation covered by none of the hypotheses in the main paper. Aitamurto and Lewis thus extend the research of Wulf and Blohm by highlighting this additional value creation effect.

6.3   Future research

There is a number of potential aspects that could further the research. First, the API *diffusion* as defined by the authors was solely measured in terms of adaption and awareness within the developer community. An arguably equally interesting variable would be the extent of actual usage such as the number of end consumers and API calls or the traffic driven by active customers. For owners of *me-*

diation services and *open asset services*, the popularity among users is a defining success factor of an API which is not measured by the authors. The usage volume is furthermore directly related to the potential revenue and thus an omitted variable in the regression analyses. Further research could capture that variable dependent on API *archetype* and *value creation mechanism*.

The second aspect addresses exactly those mechanisms. One can argue that both types of *economies of scope* are too loosely defined in the paper. The authors briefly explain that *economies of scope in production* occur when the production of two products is jointly less costly than separately, and *economies of scope in innovation* when the innovation of two products is jointly less costly than separately. However, a distinct differentiation between both mechanisms is lacking. This is also apparent from the six survey questions (see Table 4 in the appendix) used to determine which value creation mechanism is targeted. The hypotheses require that any API be in either *economies of scope,* while it is not unreasonable to assume that an API provider may fulfill all six conditions. In that case, the API would act within both value creation mechanisms, which is not considered by the authors. A further paper could define the mechanisms in greater detail and also provide recommendations in which ways the providers can adjust their targeted *economies of scope* in order to increase *ROI* or *diffusion*.

Another potential extension of the research concerns the classification of *mediation services*. These APIs can take shape in two ways: as an innovation platform for developers to create complementary offerings in extension to the core application or as an intermediator between two sides of a market, such as buyer and seller. Both API types differ fundamentally in their business concepts – the former strives to increase the overall value proposition of a main product while the latter generates income by charging either or both sides of the platform. A possible explanation for the absence of differentiation is the approach of studying only individual APIs. This disregards the possibility of multiple APIs on a platform with two or more connected parties, such as two-sided business marketplaces. Future research could introduce a distinction between both types, resulting in four API *archetypes*.

7 Conclusion

To conclude, the research conducted by Wulf and Blohm yields findings regarding the *ROI* and the *diffusion* of an API depending on the *archetype* and *value creation mechanism*. Both the theoretical derivations and the results of the regressions show that the observed factors cause a significant effect on the performance outcome. The provider of an API must deliberately align the design with the *value creation mechanism* to achieve a given business objective. This is exemplified by a case study on open banking at the Hellenic Bank (Kyprianides 2018) and further discussed on the basis of two closely related papers (Aitamurto and Lewis 2013; Tan et al. 2020). This paper also highlights the measurement of actual end consumer usage, a more refined definition of the *value creation mechanisms* and a further differentiation within *mediation services* as potential areas of future research.

References

Adner, R., and Kapoor, R. 2010. "Value Creation in Innovation Ecosystems: How the Structure of Technological Interdependence Affects Firm Performance in New Technology Generations," *Strategic Management Journal* (31:3), pp. 306–333.

Aitamurto, T., and Lewis, S. C. 2013. "Open Innovation in Digital Journalism: Examining the Impact of Open APIs at Four News Organizations," *New Media & Society* (15:2), pp. 314–331.

Benlian, A., Hilkert, D., and Hess, T. 2015. "How Open Is This Platform? The Meaning and Measurement of Platform Openness from the Complementors' Perspective," *Journal of Information Technology* (30:3), pp. 209–228.

Benlian, A., Koufaris, M., and Hess, T. 2011. "Service Quality in Software-as-a-Service: Developing the SaaS-Qual Measure and Examining Its Role in Usage Continuance," *Journal of Management Information Systems* (28:3), pp. 85–126.

Benzell, S., Hersh, J. S., Van Alstyne, M. W., and Lagarda, G. 2019. "The Paradox of Openness: Exposure vs. Efficiency of APIs," SSRN Scholarly Paper No. ID 3432591, Rochester, NY: Social Science Research Network.

Bodle, R. 2011. "Regimes of Sharing," *Information, Communication & Society* (14:3), Routledge, pp. 320–337.

Chesbrough, H. W., and Appleyard, M. M. 2007. "Open Innovation and Strategy," *California Management Review* (50:1), pp. 57–76.

Constantinides, P., Henfridsson, O., and Parker, G. G. 2018. "Introduction—Platforms and Infrastructures in the Digital Age," *Information Systems Research* (29:2), pp. 381–400.

Curbera, F., Khalaf, R., Mukhi, N., Tai, S., and Weerawarana, S. 2003. "The next Step in Web Services," *Communications of the ACM* (46:10), pp. 29–34.

Demirkan, H., and Delen, D. 2013. "Leveraging the Capabilities of Service-Oriented Decision Support Systems: Putting Analytics and Big Data in Cloud," *Decision Support Systems* (55:1), pp. 412–421.

Farrow, G. S. D. 2020. "Open Banking: The Rise of the Cloud Platform," *Journal of Payments Strategy & Systems* (14:2), pp. 128–146.

Farrow, G. S. D. 2020. "An Application Programming Interface Model for Open Banking Ecosystems," *Journal of Payments Strategy & Systems* (14:1), pp. 75–91.

Gawer, A. 2014. "Bridging Differing Perspectives on Technological Platforms: Toward an Integrative Framework," *Research Policy* (43:7), pp. 1239–1249.

Ghazawneh, A., and Henfridsson, O. 2013. "Balancing Platform Control and External Contribution in Third-Party Development: The Boundary Resources Model," *Information Systems Journal* (23:2), pp. 173–192.

Graph API. *Facebook for Developers*. Retrieved January 11, 2021, from https://developers.facebook.com/docs/graph-api/overview/

Harrell, F. 2015. *Regression Modeling Strategies: With Applications to Linear Models, Logistic and Ordinal Regression, and Survival Analysis*, (2nd ed.), Cham, Switzerland: Springer International Publishing.

Henfridsson, O., and Bygstad, B. 2013. "The Generative Mechanisms of Digital Infrastructure Evolution," *MIS Quarterly* (37:3), pp. 907–931.

Im, S., and Workman, J. 2004. "Market Orientation, Creativity, and New Product Performance in High-Technology Firms," *Journal of Marketing* (68:2), pp. 114–132.

Iyer, B., and Subramaniam, M. 2015. "The Strategic Value of APIs," *Harvard Business Review*. Retrieved January 10, 2021, from https://hbr.org/2015/01/the-strategic-value-of-apis

Krishnan, V., and Gupta, S. 2001. "Appropriateness and Impact of Platform-Based Product Development," *Management Science* (47:1), pp. 52–68.

Kuk, G., and Davies, T. 2011. "The Roles of Agency and Artifacts in Assembling Open Data Complementarities," in *International Conference on Information Systems*, Shanghai, China, pp. 1–16.

Kyprianides, N. 2018. "Banks, Be Bold! A Step-by-Step Guide to Moving from Legacy to Open Banking," *Journal of Digital Banking* (3:1), pp. 51–58.

Lee, D., and Seung, H. 2001. "Algorithms for Non-Negative Matrix Factorization," *Advances in Neural Information Processing Systems* (13), pp. 556–562.

Leisch, F. 2006. "A Toolbox for K-Centroids Cluster Analysis," *Computational Statistics & Data Analysis* (51:2), pp. 526–544.

Lin, A., and Chen, N.-C. 2012. "Cloud Computing as an Innovation: Perception, Attitude, and Adoption," *International Journal of Information Management* (32:6), pp. 533–540.

Niculescu, M. F., Wu, D. J., and Xu, L. 2018. "Strategic Intellectual Property Sharing: Competition on an Open Technology Platform Under Network Effects," *Information Systems Research* (29:2), pp. 498–519.

Nuettgens, M., and Iskender, D. M. A. 2008. "Business Models of Service-Oriented Information Systems - a Strategic Approach towards the Commercialization of Web Services," *Wirtschaftsinformatik* (50:1), pp. 31–38.

NYT Developer Network. Retrieved January 11, 2021, from https://developer.nytimes.com/

Panzar, J., And Willig, R. 1981. "Economies of Scope," *American Economic Review* (71:2), pp. 268–272.

Parker, G., and Van Alstyne, M. 2005. "Two-Sided Network Effects: A Theory of Information Product Design," *Management Science* (51:10), pp. 1494–1504.

Podsakoff, P., MacKenzie, S., Lee, J., and Podsakoff, N. 2003. "Common Method Biases in Behavioral Research: A Critical Review of the Literature and Recommended Remedies," *Journal of Applied Psychology* (88:5), pp. 879–903.

ProgrammableWeb Research Center. Retrieved January 11, 2021, from https://www.programmableweb.com/api-research

Rudmark, D. 2013. "The Practices of Unpaid Third-Party Developers–Implications for API Design," in *Americas Conference on Information Systems,* Chicago, USA, pp. 1–8

Setia, P., Rajagopalan, B., Sambamurthy, V., and Calantone, R. 2012. "How Peripheral Developers Contribute to Open-Source Software Development," *Information Systems Research* (23:1), pp. 144–163.

Smedlund, A. 2012. "Value Cocreation in Service Platform Business Models," *Service Science* (4:1), pp. 79–88.

Song, P., Xue, L., Rai, A., and Zhang, C. 2018. "The Ecosystem of Software Platform: A Study of Asymmetric Cross-Side Network Effects and Platform Governance," *MIS Quarterly* (42:1), pp. 121–142.

Song, P., Xue, L., Zhang, C., and Rai, A. 2017. "APIs in Software Platform: Implications for Innovation and Imitation," in *International Conference on Information Systems,* Seoul, Korea, pp. 1–11

Tan, B., Anderson, E. G., and Parker, G. G. 2020. "Platform Pricing and Investment to Drive Third-Party Value Creation in Two-Sided Networks," *Information Systems Research* (31:1), pp. 217–239.

Tiwana, A., Konsynski, B., and Bush, A. A. 2010. "Platform Evolution: Coevolution of Platform Architecture, Governance, and Environmental Dynamics," *Information Systems Research* (21:4), pp. 675–687.

Wulf, J., and Blohm, I. 2020. "Fostering Value Creation with Digital Platforms: A Unified Theory of the Application Programming Interface Design," *Journal of Management Information Systems* (37:1), pp. 251–281.

Xin, M., and Levina, N. 2008. "Software-as-a-Service Model: Elaborating Client-Side Adoption Factors," in *International Conference on Information Systems,* Paris, France, pp. 1–12.

Xue, L., Rai, A., Song, P., and Cheng, Z. 2017. "Third-Party Developers' Adoption of APIs and Their Continued New App Development in Software Platform: A Competing Risk Analysis," in *Conference on Information Systems & Technology,* Houston, USA, pp. 1–19

Yoo, Y., Henfridsson, O., and Lyytinen, K. 2010. "The New Organizing Logic of Digital Innovation: An Agenda for Information Systems Research," *Information Systems Research* (21:4), pp. 724–735.

Zachariadis, M., and Ozcan, P. 2016. "The API Economy and Digital Transformation in Financial Services: The Case of Open Banking," *SSRN Electronic Journal.*

Zimmermann, S., Mueller, M., and Heinrich, B. 2016. "Exposing and Selling the Use of Web Services–an Option to Be Considered in Make-or-Buy Decision-Making," *Decision Support Systems* (89), pp. 28–40.

Abbreviations

AISP	Account Information Service Provider
ASPSP	Account Servicing Payments Service Providers
API	Application Programming Interface
ERP	Enterprise-Resource-Planning System
IT	Information Technology
IS	Information Systems
PISP	Payment Initiation Provider
PSD2	Revised Payment Services Directive
ROI	Return on Investment
TPP	Third-party providers

Appendix

A1 Platform and API characteristics

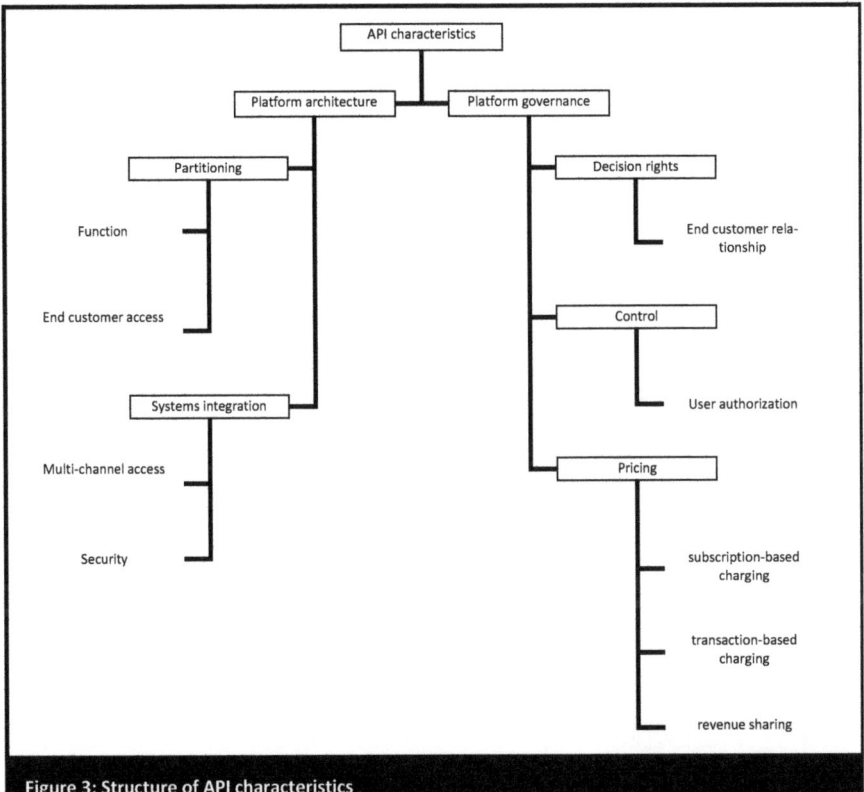

Figure 3: Structure of API characteristics based on Wulf and Blohm (2020)

A2 Full research process

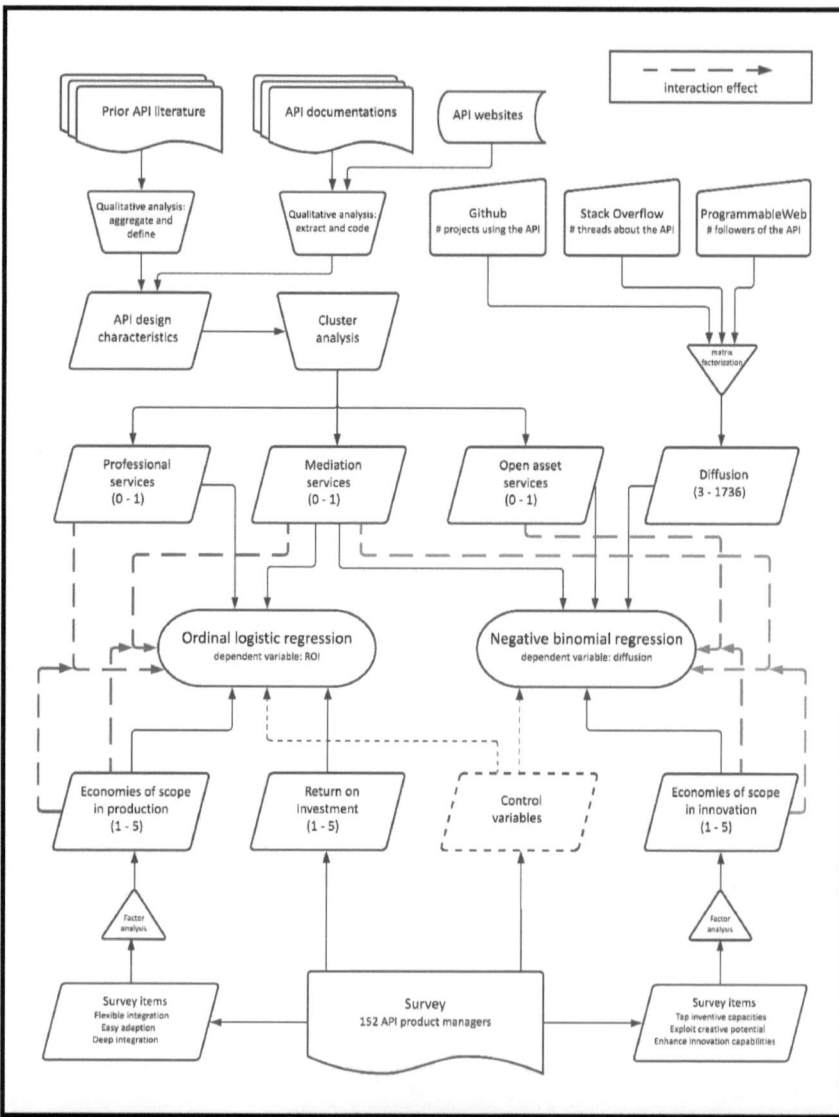

Figure 4: Research process in full

based on Wulf & Blohm (2020)

A3 Regression analysis results

Table 2. Ordinal logistic regression results
adapted from Wulf and Blohm (2020)

Variables	Model 1a API ROI (main effects)		Model 1b API ROI (full model)	
	Coefficients	Exp(β) (Odd Ratio)	Coefficients	Exp(β) (Odd Ratio)
Economies of scope in production	0.20 (0.19)	1.23	0.23 (0.2)	1.26
Similarity professional service archetype	0.12 (0.16)	1.13	0.16 (0.17)	1.17
Similarity mediation archetype	-0.16 (0.16)	0.85	-0.23 (0.17)	0.79
H1 Economies of scope in production * similarity professional services archetype			0.45** (0.18)	1.57
H2 Economies of scope in production * similarity mediation archetype			0.37* (0.18)	1.45
Functional quality	1.15** (0.23)	3.14	1.17** (0.24)	3.22
Service innovativeness	-0.08* (0.00)	0.66	-0.37 (0.20)	0.69
Employees API provider	-0.06 (0.13)	0.95	-0.07 (0.14)	0.93
Respondent API Affiliation	0.72 (0.47)	2.06	0.71 (0.48)	2.04
Respondent years API provider	0.01 (0.16)	1.01	-0.03 (0.16)	0.97
R2	0.26		0.30	
Δ R2			0.04*	

Notes: **p < 0.01, * < 0.05; N = 152; ROI = Return on Investment; Reported are standardized beta values; Standard errors in parentheses

Table 3. Negative binomial regression results
adapted from Wulf and Blohm (2020)

Variables	Model 2a API Diffusion (main effects)		Model 2b API Diffusion (full model)	
	Coefficients	Exp(β) (Odd Ratio)	Coefficients	Exp(β) (Odd Ratio)
Economies of scope in innovation	-0.34 (0.26)	0.71	-0.32 (0.22)	0.72
Similarity mediation archetype	-0.08 (0.23)	0.92	0.00 (0.19)	1.00
Similarity open asset archetype	-0.22 (0.22)	0.80	-0.24 (0.19)	0.79
H3 Economies of scope in innovation * similarity open services archetype			0.45* (0.22)	1.57
H4 Economies of scope in innovation * similarity mediation archetype			0.07 (0.2)	1.08
Functional quality	0.29 (0.28)	1.33	0.29 (0.24)	1.33
Service innovativeness	0.01 (0.29)	1.01	-0.02 (0.24)	0.98
Employees API provider	0.35 (0.21)	1.42	0.36* (0.18)	1.43
Respondent API Affiliation	-1.19 (0.65)	0.30	-1.14 (0.63)	0.32
Respondent years API provider	-0.11 (0.22)	0.90	-0.07 (0.19)	0.94
R2	0.25		0.30	
Δ R2			0.05**	

Notes: **p < 0.01, * < 0.05; N = 152; Reported are standardized beta values; Standard errors in parentheses

A4 Survey questions regarding economies of scope

Table 4: Excerpt of the survey instrument regarding value creation mechanisms adapted from Wulf and Blohm (2020)

	Please indicate the extent to which the following statements describe your company's API strategy (1: not at all - 5: to a very large extent).
Economies of scope in production	By modularizing our IT resources (applications, data, or infrastructure) and providing API access to modules, ... • (prod_1) we allow flexible integration of our IT resources into an external developer's IT system. • (prod_2) we facilitate adaptation of our IT resources to an external developer's IT system. • (prod_3) we enable deep integration of our IT resources into an external developer's IT system.
Economies of scope in innovation	By exposing internal IT resources (applications, data, or infrastructure) to external developers, ... • (inno_1) we tap into the inventive capacities of the external developer community. • (inno_2) we exploit the creative potential of external developers. • (inno_3) we enhance our innovation capabilities.

A5 Literature search process and scope amendment

Because of the actuality of the main paper, only little development can be found on the specific re-search topic of performance effects subject to API design types as of now. As further research was very sparsely available in existing literature, the scope of the subchapter *Role in discourse* was amended on January 5ᵗʰ 2021 in consultation with Dr. Mrass. The question was now allowed to ex-pand on topics without immediate relation to the main paper (e.g. direct citations), and the included papers could have been published prior to the main paper. Dr. Mrass also permitted the use of a book of the Springer Verlag and the webpage ProgrammableWeb as sources.

Regarding the choice of further literature, some papers were included despite not being in a highly rated journal: Bodle, 2011 was published in *Information, Communication and Society*, which is not represented in the VHB Jourqual, but the paper is so far cited 124 times. Therefore, academic rele-vance was assumed. Aitmaturo, 2013, published in New Media & Society (also not in the VHB Jour-qual) is cited 117 times. The journal is also ranked 7ᵗʰ of 445 Communication journals listed on Sci-mago Journal Rank. Zachariadis, 2016 was found in the SSRN Electronic Journal (which is not in the VHB Jourqual) and is cited 60 times, which was also deemed significant enough to be included.

The following search strings were used to find API-related articles in highly rated journals. The same searches were conducted with *Open Banking* AND *API* to find papers in IS literature for the *Practical example* subchapter, which unfortunately did not yield any viable results. Therefore, the papers in the *Journal of Digital Banking* were included because of very high content-related fit.

Web of Science	Proquest
PUBLICATION NAME: ("Information Systems Re-search" OR "MIS Quarterly" OR "Journal of Man-agement Information Systems" OR "Journal of the Association for Information Systems" OR "Journal of Information Technology" OR "Pro-ceedings of the International Conference on In-formation Systems" OR "Information Systems Journal" OR "The Journal of Strategic Information Systems" OR "European Journal of Information Systems" OR "INFORMS Journal on Computing" OR "SIAM Journal on Computing") AND ALL FIELDS: ("application programming interface")	pub("Information Systems Research" OR "MIS Quarterly" OR "Journal of Management Infor-mation Systems" OR "Journal of the Association for Information Systems" OR "Journal of Infor-mation Technology" OR "Proceedings of the In-ternational Conference on Information Systems" OR "Information Systems Journal" OR "The Jour-nal of Strategic Information Systems" OR "Euro-pean Journal of Information Systems" OR "IN-FORMS Journal on Computing" OR "SIAM Journal on Computing") AND ("application programming interface" OR "API")

A5 Literature not included in the paper

The following sources were considered for inclusion in the paper because of high relevance for the discussion but were eventually disregarded due to space constraints.

Acker, A., and Kreisberg, A. 2020. "Social Media Data Archives in an API-Driven World," *Archival Science*, pp. 105–123.

Bahri, G., and Lobo, T. 2021. "The Seven Highly Effective Strategies to Survive in the Open Banking World," *Journal of Digital Banking* (5:2), pp. 102–109.

Basole, R. C. 2019. "On the Evolution of Service Ecosystems: A Study of the Emerging API Economy," in *Handbook of Service Science, Volume II*, Cham, Switzerland: Springer International Publishing, pp. 479–495.

Berger, T., Chen, C., and Frey, C. B. 2018. "Drivers of Disruption? Estimating the Uber Effect," *European Economic Review* (110), pp. 197–210.

De Vidts, G. 2020. "Application Programming Interfaces: The New (Old) Game in Town," *Journal of Securities Operations & Custody* (12:3), pp. 278–285.

González-Mora, C., Garrigós, I., and Zubcoff, J. 2020. "A Universal Application Programming Interface to Access and Reuse Linked Open Data," in *Web Engineering*, Cham, Switzerland: Springer International Publishing, pp. 556–560.

Karhu, K., Gustafsson, R., Eaton, B., Henfridsson, O., and Sørensen, C. 2020. "Four Tactics for Implementing a Balanced Digital Platform Strategy," *MIS Quarterly Executive* (19:2), pp. 105–120.

Karhu, K., Gustafsson, R., and Lyytinen, K. 2018. "Exploiting and Defending Open Digital Platforms with Boundary Resources: Android's Five Platform Forks," *Information Systems Research* (29:2), pp. 479–497.

Lahiri, A., Dewan, R. M., and Freimer, M. 2010. "The Disruptive Effect of Open Platforms on Markets for Wireless Services," *Journal of Management Information Systems* (27:3), pp. 81–110.

Lindman, J., Horkoff, J., Hammouda, I., and Knauss, E. 2020. "Emerging Perspectives of Application Programming Interface Strategy: A Framework to Respond to Business Concerns," *IEEE Software* (37:2), pp. 52–59.

Mishra, M. 2020. "Evolution of the Invisible Bank: How Partnerships with FinTechs Are Driving Digital Innovation," *Journal of Digital Banking* (5:1), pp. 36–40.

Ofoeda, J. 2020. "Exploring Value Creation Through Application Programming Interfaces: A Developing Economy Perspective", in *Handbook of Research on Managing Information Systems in Developing Economies*, Ghana: IGI Global, pp. 295–316.

Ofoeda, J., Boateng, R., and Effah, J. 2019. "Application Programming Interface (API) Research: A Review of the Past to Inform the Future," *International Journal of Enterprise Information Systems (IJEIS)* (15:3), IGI Global, pp. 76–95.

Ofoeda, J., Boateng, R., and Effah, J. 2020. *Achieving Organizational Agility through Application Programming Interfaces: The Effect of Dynamic Capability and Institutional Forces*, CONF-IRM 2020 Proceedings, December 1.

Rabhi, F. A., Bandara, M., Lu, K., and Dewan, S. 2021. "Design of an Innovative IT Platform for Analytics Knowledge Management," *Future Generation Computer Systems* (116), pp. 209–219.

Vaccari, L., Posada, M., Gattwinkel, D., Friis-Christensen, A., and Nativi, S. 2020. "Application Programming Interfaces in Governments: Why, What and How.", Luxembourg: Publications Office of the European Union

Venkatesh, V., Bala, H., and Sambamurthy, V. 2016. "Implementation of an Information and Communication Technology in a Developing Country: A Multimethod Longitudinal Study in a Bank in India," *Information Systems Research* (27:3), pp. 558–579.

Wadsworth, J. 2020. "Readying the Open Banking System for Success," *Journal of Digital Banking* (5:1), pp. 6–12.

Zhou, M., Geng, D., Abhishek, V., and Li, B. 2020. "When the Bank Comes to You: Branch Network and Customer Omnichannel Banking Behavior," *Information Systems Research*, pp. 176–197.

YOUR KNOWLEDGE HAS VALUE

- We will publish your bachelor's and master's thesis, essays and papers

- Your own eBook and book - sold worldwide in all relevant shops

- Earn money with each sale

Upload your text at www.GRIN.com and publish for free